Parenting

BASICS EVERY PARENT NEEDS TO KNOW

LAURA PHILLIPS

BALBOA.PRESS

A DIVISION OF HAY HOUSE

Balboa Press books may be ordered through booksellers or by contacting:

Balboa Press
A Division of Hay House
1663 Liberty Drive
Bloomington, IN 47403
www.balboapress.com
844-682-1282

Because of the dynamic nature of the Internet, any web addresses or links contained in this book may have changed since publication and may no longer be valid. The views expressed in this work are solely those of the author and do not necessarily reflect the views of the publisher, and the publisher hereby disclaims any responsibility for them.

The author of this book does not dispense medical advice or prescribe the use of any technique as a form of treatment for physical, emotional, or medical problems without the advice of a physician, either directly or indirectly. The intent of the author is only to offer information of a general nature to help you in your quest for emotional and spiritual well-being. In the event you use any of the information in this book for yourself, which is your constitutional right, the author and the publisher assume no responsibility for your actions.

Print information available on the last page.

ISBN: 978-1-9822-3772-1 (sc)
ISBN: 978-1-9822-3774-5 (hc)
ISBN: 978-1-9822-3773-8 (e)

Library of Congress Control Number: 2019917166

Balboa Press rev. date: 02/23/2021

Contents

What is Parenting?

Parenting is using basic skills or rules that can be learned.

Parenting can seem overwhelming. Many parents wonder what is the right thing to do. What if I make mistakes? Will I cause damage? Will I default to the things my parents did, even the things I swore I would never do?

Guess what? You will make mistakes. You will default to what your parents did. Everyone makes mistakes and that is okay.

However, there are tried and true guidelines, or "proper" parenting techniques backed by research that you can learn. And you can still fix things if you make a mistake.

Become aware of what you liked and did not like in your parents' parenting. Then you can choose to repeat the good things and consciously replace the rest with the parenting basics presented here.

If you parent from a place of love, and understand your job is to set and reinforce age appropriate rules and teach life skills in a respectful, caring, firm manner, you will be fine.

Read on to understand how to do this.

The Basics – What Do I Do to Be a Good Parent?

Guidance

Part of a parent's role is to teach children how to think on their own and how to grow up to be happy self-sufficient adults who can engage in healthy relationships.

Setting the Rules

A parents' role is to set appropriate rules and boundaries that keep the child safe; physically and emotionally.

Children need to know their parent is setting the rules in a fair and predictable manner and is in charge. This provides the child with a sense of emotional and physical security.

Teaching Skills

Your job is to be a parent, not a buddy.

Laughing, playing and having fun with your children is important and teaches them how to have joy. However, the parenting role must remain the primary goal. A parent's role is to teach skill development such as how to do tasks, how to deal with emotions and relationships and how to deal with problems and challenges.

Building Self Esteem

Your job as a parent is to develop your child's sense of value and self love.

The key is:

Love and Limits

Be Firm and Loving.

The optimal parenting is a mix of love, acceptance, and setting and reinforcing age appropriate limits. Being overly restrictive or punitive can limit healthy skill development and self-esteem. Being overly permissive without limits can result in uncontrolled, impulsive, self centered behaviours which will eventually result in a loss of self-esteem and life direction.

Setting the Rules and Reinforcing with Consequences

Be Clear. Explain the Rules and Why They are Important.

Your child needs to know what is expected and what is not allowed. This needs to be clear.

Children need to understand why the rules are important and meaningful to them.

Use Consequences as Punishment

(instead of yelling or being physical)

When your child does not do what is expected or does something they have been told not to, use consequences.

Be Clear About the Consequences

For example, you asked your child to take out the garbage a few times and it is not done. Tell your child a consequence will happen if the garbage is not taken out by a certain time. A consequence could be that the phone will be taken away for the next two hours.

Be Consistent with Reinforcing Consequences

Follow through with what you say.

If you warn there will be consequences for behaviours done/not done – make sure you give the consequences.

If you tell your child a consequence will be given, it is very important to follow through. If you do not, your child will learn that you do not mean what you say and will tend not to listen to you or take what you say seriously.

If you consistently do not follow through, you will lose your child's respect.

When this happens repeatedly, over time, generally the child will start to lose respect for others and themselves. They will not listen to rules, and will start to get in situations where they get in trouble as they have not learned their behaviours come with consequences. They may develop impulse control problems; difficulty setting personal limits and making safe or healthy decisions. They are now geared for immediate gratification which means they will tend to do what they want when they want to, regardless of the consequences. These decisions will likely not be healthy decisions as they are not considering the positive or negative ripple effects of their actions. This could result in problematic substance use or risky relationship behaviours over time.

Ensure the Consequences are Suitable for the Behaviour

Consider whether the consequences fit the behaviour. Try not to set consequences when you are angry as they may be more severe than needed.

For example, if you come home stressed from work, and your child did not take out the garbage, you may be so angry that you ground your child for a month. However, the punishment is usually losing the phone for two hours. You can correct your mistake by telling your child you overreacted and are sticking with the usual punishment.

The two skills: 1) admitting you made a mistake, and 2) fixing it – are important for your child to learn. These skills are taught as your children will model your behaviour.

Children vary in personality and in needs, so your consequences should be appropriate for your child. For example, a child with autism will have different levels of understanding and may need different approaches.

Think About the Cause of the Misbehaviour

Keep in mind that sometimes children misbehave to get attention.

If you see a pattern of acting out or new misbehaviours, pay attention. Changes in behaviours can be warning signs.

Think about the amount of positive attention you are giving them. Sometimes children just need to know you see and hear them. If children are not getting enough attention, they may start to act out to get your attention.

For children negative interaction is better than no interaction.

Be Aware of Changes in Your Child's Behaviour

If a child is being bullied, intimidated, sexually abused or threatened in any way, or if there is a lot of conflict in the home, this will usually be reflected in changes in your child's behaviours.

Changes in behaviours can show up as changes in personality such as irritability, anger, mood swings, withdrawal, acting out with verbal or physical aggression or changes in attendance or participation in school and social activities.

Speak to your child about what is going on. Listen in a non-judgemental, accepting way. Help your child understand there are ways to deal with every situation. Help your child problem-solve while being supportive and non-judgemental. Seek counselling if needed.

Set Age Appropriate Limits

It is the child's job to explore in order to learn necessary skills.

For example, a toddler does not know it is dangerous to stick a finger in the electrical socket. It is the parent's job to keep the fingers away from the socket, while encouraging the child to explore.

For example, an older child may not want to come in when you call them. It is important to teach them they need to come in when called for reasons of safety and respect. Use a consequence such as losing some TV or computer time. By using consequences to ensure they understand the boundaries and rules, you are less likely to have to deal with teenagers who do not respect rules.

Consequences for teenagers could be taking away their phone or grounding for a certain period of time. It is more difficult to reinforce consequences with teenagers if they were not raised with consistent consequences. However, it is never too late to start. Initially a teenager who has not had consequences consistently will rebel. If you are consistently firm and caring when setting and reinforcing the consequences, they will learn you mean business and will start to respect you and your rules.

Children need limits that are age-appropriate but allow them to grow.

Give Choices Instead of Saying No

Gives choices and alternatives.

This helps a child learn to think and problem-solve.

This allows your children to learn how to make decisions and how to trust their judgement.

And, when saying no is necessary, it is meaningful and listened to.

For example, say "we cannot play with that toy now as it has small parts and the baby can choke. You can play with this toy now. When your brother takes his nap, we will play with that toy".

Focus on the Behaviour, Not the Child

Children need to understand their behaviour is wrong, that they are not a bad person. It is important to emphasize the behaviour is bad, not that the child is bad.

For example, try not to say "you are a bad boy, what is wrong with you?". Instead say "knocking over your brother's sandcastle is not okay. Say you are sorry and help your brother build back the sandcastle". If he refuses, tell him what the consequences will be; for example, no television that night.

If a child grows up being told they are bad, the child will grow up thinking they are a bad person. If they think they are a bad person, it is more likely they will behave badly.

It is important to let your child know you still love them, **and** they are still getting consequences for their behaviour.

Give Your Child Time to Calm Down

Provide a cooling off period if needed for you or your child.

Your child may feel embarrassed or ashamed for their behaviour. Give them time to calm down. Talk to them.

Teach your child how to calm down.

For example, say something like "when I am frustrated, I sit down and take a few deep breaths. Why don't you go to the other room, take some deep breaths, calm down and then when you are ready, we can talk".

If you, the parent, are feeling angry, this is a good time for some deep breaths of your own.

Why Does Physical Punishment Not Work

What you do to a child, is what they learn to do.

For example, if you yell or hit a child when you are angry at them, they will model your behaviour and yell or hit when angry.

Physical punishment may get the child to do what you want them to do. But it may make them angry and they may act out against you or someone else which will lead to negative consequences. Physical punishment may also lead to the child not doing what they have been asked next time as they are angry about the physical act.

Repeated Verbal Abuse and/ or Physical Punishment has Serious Long-Term Effects

Repeated yelling or physical punishment will make the child feel unsafe, angry or scared, and will make your relationship worse. It will also set the child up for problems in future relationships as they will be at risk of being emotionally or physically abused or could end up being an abuser.

The more a child is neglected or abused – yelled at, called names, put down, made fun of, hit, or shamed – the child will grow up feeling they do not deserve to be treated well. They may feel anger and act out towards others. Or they may feel they deserve to be treated badly, have reduced self-esteem and end up in relationships where they are treated badly or engage in self-harming behaviours, drug use or put themselves in risky relationships or situations.

Skill Development

Encourage Your Child to Try New Things

This is how they develop skills. This is how they learn.

Try not to hover or be over-protective. This creates anxiety in the child.

Encourage your child to try new skills.

For example, let them try to figure out the new game and then help when they need it or ask for help.

Teach a new skill and let your child try it. Stand back and watch, or stand by guiding step by step, whichever seems needed or requested by the child. Use encouraging words such as "you can do it, try it like this, that's good".

Ensure the skill is manageable and age appropriate.

Do not expect perfection, especially when learning a new skill. Expecting perfection will make a child feel they are underperforming, and perhaps feel as if they are disappointing you. This will make the child doubt their ability to do the task well, and may lesson enthusiasm or desire to try the task again or even try another new task.

Teach Your Child How To Learn and Work Through Frustration

An important part of learning is being able to work through feelings of frustration when something is not understood or is difficult.

Encourage your child to work through their frustration when learning something new.

Show them how to do this.

Do not put them down for being frustrated. Normalize the frustration. Tell them it is normal to feel frustrated at different points when learning something new.

Teach them how to step back, take a few breaths and re-examine the situation or try a new approach in order to work through their frustration.

Show Your Child That Trying Again is How We Learn

Remind your child that we learn when we try.

Doing something over and over is how we learn and how we get better at the task.

Accountability

Let Your Children Make and Fix Minor Mistakes

This is how they learn lessons and how to fix situations. This is how they learn that their actions have consequences and how others are affected. This is how they learn to accept responsibility for their actions.

For example, if your child spills milk, have the child help clean up the spill. No need to shame or make them feel bad by yelling, saying what is wrong with you, or look what you have done.

Just have them help you clean it up. Let them know it is okay; accidents happen.

Staying Calm Helps Your Child Understand that Mistakes are Part of Life

Sometimes an accident will happen after you asked your child to be careful. Even if you feel frustrated, stay calm. Your child will realize the mistake and it will not be useful if you shame them or put them down.

Support them by teaching them how to fix it.

Allow Your Child to Grow Up

Allow your child to make choices and minor mistakes and to feel the consequences – keeping in mind what is age appropriate. Help guide them through different ways to fix the mistakes.

This may be hard for you to do, but it is necessary for your child's healthy development.

If you do everything for your child, they will not learn to do things themselves.

Co-dependence and Enabling – What is This?

A simplified explanation of co-dependence and enabling is doing things for your child that they should be doing or learning to do on their own. The child learns to rely on the parent to do things for them. This is at the expense of the child learning what they need to learn to become a healthy, independently functioning adult. When you continue to do for them instead of supporting them in developing skills to do on their own, you are enabling them to be dependent on you. This diminishes your child's growth, maturity and sense of self-esteem. Your child will feel an excessive need to rely on others to do for them.

For example: A youth starts using drugs affecting the child's ability to focus and finish homework. The child starts skipping school. The parent lies to the school and makes up false reasons for the child not attending. The parent starts doing the homework.

This is enabling as the parent covers up by lying and not having the child be held accountable for their behaviours. The parent allows the child to continue using drugs, skipping school and avoiding homework without any negative consequences such as getting in trouble at school. The parent may be telling the child to stop using drugs and to stop skipping school. However, if the parent is not using consequences to address the negative behaviours and is not addressing the emotional issues behind the change in behaviour then telling the child to stop will not be effective.

The enabling by the parent creates a situation where the child ends up not learning the necessary skills in school, and does not learn how to accept responsibility. Also, the enabling is not addressing the reasons why the child felt a need to start taking drugs – what emotional or social situation is the child avoiding with the drug use? This needs to be addressed.

Co-dependency is behind this strategy – the parent feels needed and becomes overinvolved in an unhealthy way. The parent mistakenly believes the role of the parent is to cover up the child's mistakes, or pick up the pieces for them. The child's development of social and emotional skills is hindered, and the child remains dependent on the parent in the long run.

It is not the role of the parent to cover up a child's mistakes or enable the child to avoid taking responsibility.

It is the role of the parent to teach the child how to fix mistakes and take accountability for their words and actions.

Teach Your Child That
Apologies are Important

If your child engages in behaviours that purposely or accidently hurt someone or someone's belongings, hold your child accountable. Explain to your child the consequences of their actions, and help them problem-solve through ways they can make things right.

For example, have your child apologize to the person and accompany them for support. If there is damaged property have the child pay with money from their allowance. This teaches the child to learn how to take responsibility for their actions, to develop compassion for other people's feelings, to be able to develop the skills to problem-solve, and repair relationships and make things right.

Show Your Child that Adults Also Apologize and Are Accountable

Ensure your child hears you apologize when you have done something wrong.

For example, if you are rude to someone or if you insist you are right, but find out you are wrong, apologize.

Ensure you apologize to your children when you have done something that hurts them in some way. For example, if you spoke to them harshly or embarrassed them.

Apologizing is not a sign of weakness. It means you are accepting responsibility for your behaviour and is a sign of strength.

Teach your Children to Navigate Difficult Situations – to say no when threatened or put in an uncomfortable situation

Teach your children to be assertive and how to set boundaries.

If you never let them say no, they won't know how.

Teach your children to listen to their feelings and that they have a right to get out of a situation if they are feeling uncomfortable or scared.

It is important to listen to your children when they feel unsafe, and to deal with and/or remove them from an unsafe situation. This teaches children/teens they have the right to say no in order to protect themselves when in an uncomfortable or threatening situation. This includes the right to address threatening or bullying words or behaviours, as well as physical, emotional and sexual abuse.

It is important to teach your child how to be assertive and how to listen and respect their gut instinct when something is wrong to be able to keep themselves safe.

If you are experiencing or have experienced any of the above noted abuses, it may be difficult for you to protect your children, or teach your children how to protect themselves. It may be difficult to teach that children have the right to protect themselves if that was not done for you.

If you as a parent had a difficult time in your childhood or adulthood, such as having your emotions or needs or safety unattended to in various ways, then you will have difficulty teaching your child how to navigate difficult situations or stay safe. If you were not permitted to say no or protect yourself from abuse, you may not have the skills to teach. This is a good time to seek counselling yourself to develop these skills to be able to teach and model them for your child. This is when it is important for you to seek counselling to learn how to protect yourself and your children.

Dealing with Change

Children need to be supported through change. Teach them that change is a normal part of life. Children need to feel secure with change. Reassure them with words that they will be alright. Involve them in change, at an age appropriate level, so they feel a part of things and not fearful.

For example, if moving to a new house, get them involved and excited by asking what colours they want in their new room. Tell them about fun activities around the new home such as a splash pad or laser tag.

Validate their worries and concerns. Instead of saying there is nothing to worry about, discuss their worries and fears and help them work through them.

Most children need advance notice of even a minor change. For example, let your child know fifteen minutes in advance when it is time to stop playing, leave somewhere or go to bed. It is helpful to give five-minutes notice as well. This helps your child prepare for the change.

If children are raised to understand that change is a part of life, and taught how to adapt to change and make it advantageous, they will feel secure and comfortable with change.

Teach Your Child How to Cope with Disappointment or Things They Cannot Change

Help your child understand that part of life is not always being able to control what happens around us. We cannot control what other people do or say.

However, this does not mean that the child needs to feel out of control when disappointed or facing something they cannot change. Teach your child how to recover from disappointment and work through things they cannot change.

Teach Your Child That While They Cannot Always Control What Happens, They Can Control How They React

Show your child what they **can** do.

They can work through their feelings of disappointment by talking about the situation, and looking at options of how to deal with parts they can control.

They can always take control of their emotions by validating what they feel and self soothing and seeking support.

In life there will be times when your child is emotionally hurt. It is important to teach your child how to work through emotional pain and move forward in life. It is important that when emotionally painful things happen, we do not continue to carry the emotional pain and the emotional burden with us throughout life.

Moldy Cheese Analogy

As a therapist I repeatedly see clients who are suffering emotionally because of what someone did to them. In life there will be times when we, or our child is emotionally hurt. We, or our child may encounter physical, emotional or sexual harassment or abuse.

What is most important that when someone does something to us, that we do not continue to carry the emotional pain and the emotional burden of what they did to us. Emphasis on what they did to us. We did not do it. They did it. So here is the analogy. (Please note I heard the best analogy of what to do with emotional pain. However, I could not remember the exact example or source, so I made up my own analogy based on what I recall.)

If someone walks up to you and hands you a huge piece of moldy smelly cheese, what do you do? Do you carry it around with you? No, you throw it away.

If someone throws a huge piece of moldy cheese into your car, do you drive around with it in your car for the next twenty years? No, you address the situation by stopping the car and getting rid of the moldy cheese.

When someone abuses you physically, emotionally or sexually this is the moldy cheese they are handing you. Refuse to hold on to the moldy cheese; throw it back to them. Understand it was their behaviour. It is their shame and embarrassment to carry, not yours. Don't carry it for them. Give it back to them to carry. Throw back the moldy cheese.

It is important to understand when someone hurts you, this experience does not define who you are. You can choose not to let it. You are so much more than that negative experience.

Again, counselling can help you to understand how to do this.

This is an important concept to help your child understand so their self-esteem and sense of self worth is not lessoned by someone else's hurtful behaviour.

Building
Relationship Skills

Teach Your Child How to Navigate Relationships

Children need to know sometimes there are problems in relationships, sometimes through no fault of their own. They need to know this is not the end of the world.

Perhaps your child's best friend moved away or found another best friend. Your child needs to know this is part of life and they will make new friends. Your child needs to learn that their self-esteem does not come from who likes them or does not like them, or by who stays in their life or exits their life. Self-esteem is not formed by whether someone wants to be with them.

Children need to understand that others are not obligated to be their friend. This is an important concept to grasp so they learn to deal with disappointment in relationships later on.

Important Things to Teach Your Child About Relationships

- It is important to treat people well; the way you want to be treated.

- Anyone has the right to leave a relationship when they want. Do it kindly and honestly.

- You cannot force someone to be in a relationship with you, nor should you want to or try to.

- It is healthy to leave a relationship when being treated badly, and seek help if needed.

- The end of a relationship can hurt very badly. However, after the grieving process which you will get through, things will get better, and life continues, and may even be better.

Model the Types of Relationships You Would Like for Your Child

Ensure you have healthy and fulfilling relationships.

Ensure you are not in the type of relationships that you would not want for your child. If your child sees you being mistreated or abused, or sees you mistreating or abusing your partner, it is more than likely they will repeat the same patterns in their own relationships.

Teach Your Child How to Work Through Conflict

Teach your child that conflict is normal and expected and if worked through can make the relationship stronger. Explain that in any relationship there will be instances where people have different needs, feelings or opinions.

Teach your child to understand that they have the right to express their feelings and needs and this is healthy to do. Remind them it is important to listen to the other person's feelings and needs in a relationship as this shows the person you care about them. There is skill in finding a way to meet both sets of needs in a relationship. When done properly both people feel cared about and that they have each other's back.

Model Healthy Conflict Resolution

If you as a parent model healthy conflict resolution, the child will learn the skills.

Resolve conflict the way you want your children to resolve conflict. Use reasoning and respect to understand what the other person needs and to express your needs. Then work through various options until both people involved feel satisfied with the solution to the conflict. This process strengthens relationships.

Yelling, swearing, giving the silent treatment or avoiding the conflict only leads to breakdown of the relationship.

Trust, respect, validation and emotional safety are what feels good in a relationship and what makes the relationship healthy.

Teach Your Child to Become Aware of Their Own Feelings

It is important to teach your child (in age-appropriate terms) to listen to their feelings and what they know is appropriate and inappropriate to avoid being manipulated or being taken advantage of by others when they are trying to balance needs in a relationship.

It is teaching a mix of assertiveness and compassion.

Teach Your Child it is Not Acceptable for a Friend or Partner to Abuse Them in Any Way

If you see signs that your child is being mistreated, you need to speak to them about it. Signs of abuse could include withdrawal from friends and family, wearing dark sunglasses or covering up body parts or a change in personality or routine. Help your child learn to listen to their own feelings to understand that the mistreatment feels wrong, whether in their feelings of anxiety, fear, confusion, knot in the stomach, feeling nauseous, etc.

Teach them how to set healthy boundaries and stop the mistreatment.

Ensure they know that no one deserves to be treated badly. Discuss what a healthy relationship looks and feels like, versus an unhealthy or abusive relationship.

If you are concerned your child is in over their head and in danger – serious emotional or physical abuse or human trafficking – do what you need to do to keep your child safe. Arrange counselling, or involve the police if necessary.

Your child needs to know that they are in no way responsible for the abuse. It is not their fault. Your child needs to understand that abuse is the abuser's issue and only the abuser can work out their problems. You cannot solve someone's issues by loving them out of them, or simply by staying with them.

Be a source of support for your child. Be non-judgemental and truly listen. Make sure your child feels you hear and understand them. Ensure you do not encourage your child to stay in a harmful relationship. Do not judge them for leaving a relationship when they have their reasons. There may be things you do not know.

Teach Your Children How to Handle Challenges in Relationships

If you teach your child how to handle the ups and downs of friendship, they will be better equipped to handle the challenges of teenage and adult relationships.

If hurtful things happen in a relationship, it is important not to see the other as a bad person. It is healthier to understand people make mistakes in relationships just as you may do.

At some point your child may have their heart broken, just as they may break someone else's heart. It is important to teach that relationships do not always last and that is alright. The end of a relationship does not have to mean that there is something wrong with the other. It could be that during the relationship it was realized the two people had different interests, goals, or values and maybe were just not a good fit.

This is very different from a relationship that is controlling or abusive in any way, and requires setting boundaries and knowing you have the right to protect yourself.

Teach Your Child How to Deal with Peer Pressure

At the pre-teen/teenage stage peers become one of the strongest influencers. It is important that teenagers are given the ability to know how to say no to peer pressure and how to stay true to their own values.

For example, your teenager is out with friends and there is drinking and driving involved. If discussed in advance, and the teenager is prepared with options and support, your teenager will know they can call you and you will pick them up or get a taxi for them to come home.

It is important to positively reinforce your teenager for making a good decision to call for help to get out of a potentially dangerous situation. If the parent attacks the teenager for getting themselves in a bad situation, instead of being commended for calling for help, then the teenager is not likely to call the parent next time, and will likely remain in the risky situation. If the parent is there to help without judgement, the teenager feels safe to fall back on the parent when needed. The parent can later talk to the teenager about what happened and options for avoiding potentially dangerous situations, and/or use the opportunity to reinforce that the teenager handled the situation totally appropriately. This will accomplish enhancing your teenager's problem-solving skills, and skills to follow their own values and be able to successfully manage peer pressure.

As noted earlier self confidence and self-esteem are developed by parents having confidence in their child's abilities and decisions, as well as being there to provide love, help and support.

Dealing with Emotions

It is Important to Realize that Emotions are Healthy and Necessary. Think of Emotions as Guides Through Life

Our emotions tell us when someone is not treating us well, when something is dangerous, and when situations or people are safe.

When Parents Listen and Attend to a Child's Emotions, it Teaches the Child to Listen and Attend to Their Emotions

For example, if a child is feeling sad and the parent tells them not to feel sad then the child's feeling is de-validated (not valued, not important, shut down). If the parent listens to what the child is feeling and why and validates, the child learns their feelings are important.

Validate Your Child's Feelings

The parent can ask what is making the child feel sad, listen and tell the child that makes sense that you feel sad. The child then learns their emotions are important.

Then the parent, after giving validation, and perhaps hugging them and letting them cry, can help the child learn to shift their mood. The parent can say now that we've had a good cry, how about we go watch our favourite comedy show. That may cheer you up.

Be mindful of using a healthy way to cheer up the child; e.g. laughing, playing, going for a walk, cuddling. If you use junk food, your child may turn to junk food for comfort which may create a life long pattern.

Teach Your Children to Use Their Emotions as Guides and to Listen to Their Internal Warnings

If parents consistently de-validate a child's feeling, then the child will grow up believing their feelings are not important and will stop listening to them. As feelings are guides, not listening to the feelings can be a problem.

For example, if a teenage girl is consistently told not to feel or think a certain way, or that she is being ridiculous, then she will stop listening to her emotions and her gut instinct. If someone offers her a ride home from a party, she might accept because she is being pressured or wants to be polite. Her emotions are telling her something is wrong, as she is feeling uncomfortable. However, as she is used to having her feelings discounted, she ignores the warning signs her emotions are giving her and ends up in a dangerous situation.

Similarly, if the child was raised to be a people pleaser, and was expected to cater to everyone else's feelings and needs, the child will not listen to their own gut/emotions as they will not want to hurt anyone's feelings.

Being Comfortable with Your Own Emotions Will Be Necessary to Allow You to Guide Your Child Through Their Emotions

This can be done by seeing a counsellor or reading self help books to understand what your emotions are for and how to deal with them.

Teach Your Child to Deal with Anger in a Healthy Way

Take your child's anger seriously. Do not minimize it. Listen to it. Ask your child what is causing the anger.

Anger is a healthy emotion. Teach your child how to express anger in a healthy way. Teach your child how to express what is making them angry and how to deal with the situations that are creating the anger.

For example, your child's sibling took their toy. Your child hit the sibling and grabbed the toy back. The sibling in turn hit back and both started crying in anger.

Help the children understand it is alright to feel angry about what happened. Explain in age appropriate terms how they could have handled the situation differently.

Teach the child that if they wanted the toy, they could ask for it. If the other does not want to give it to them, they can bargain and say I will let you play with this for a while if I can play with that for a while. Or they can find something else to play with and use the other toy when the sibling is finished. Or they can tell an adult who can establish sharing rules. Explain it is not ok to hit someone or grab their things. Show what is appropriate. If the child is too young to understand the words, model the appropriate action.

Dealing with Temper Tantrums

If your child starts to try temper tantrums to get what they want, it is important to ignore the behaviour and not give them what they want. Giving in to the temper tantrum by giving what the child wants will just make the child do it more (reinforce that the temper tantrums work). If this becomes a regular parenting practice, the child will learn to have tantrums to get what they want. The child learns to manipulate the parent to get what they want which will create behavioural problems.

The parent will feel the child is out of control, when actually the parenting is out of control. It is important to nip this behaviour in the bud or it will be very stressful for the parent and the rest of the family.

Temper Tantrums Can Have a Negative Effect on Siblings

This type of situation can also be a big problem for the siblings who see the manipulative child getting away with things and getting things they were told they would not get.

The siblings see an unfair situation. Over time the co-operative siblings may start to feel angry at the unfair situation and start to develop behaviours as well. They see that tantrums can get them what they want.

Teach Calming Strategies, Coping Skills and Ways to Self Soothe

As previously noted, give your child time to calm down. Teach skills such as taking deep breaths, counting to ten before saying or doing anything and/or taking a time out.

Exercise such as walking around the block or going out in the yard can be calming. Music and art can also be calming/soothing strategies. Relaxation and meditation music and videos can be used on a regular basis to maintain a calm baseline.

The only ways your children will know how to calm or soothe themselves is by the methods you teach them. If you model unhealthy coping strategies such as aggression, alcohol or drugs, gambling, avoidance or other self-harming behaviours, then these are the coping skills which your child will learn and use.

If you model healthy coping strategies such as self care, validating emotions and problem solving through situations in healthy ways, then this is what your child will learn to do.

Teach your child when someone hurts you, you pamper yourself. When someone hurts you, you take extra special care of yourself. You do nice things that make you valued and comforted, just like you would do for someone you loved if they were hurt. Model this behaviour.

When children are hurt repeatedly, or see self-harming behaviours, they may start using self-harming thoughts or behaviours to cope.

Model and teach your child healthy ways to calm, self soothe and cope. If you notice your strategies are unhealthy you can seek counselling or educate yourself to learn new healthy ways that will help make your life better.

Think About Reasons for Behavioural or Emotional Changes

If your child is agitated or upset due to a stressful situation in the family (such as an illness or a move), it is important to notice and address what the child is feeling.

Make sure your child knows, regardless of the situation, they will be looked after. Children need to know they will be fed, taken to school and their daily routine and needs will be met.

Ensure quality time is spent with the child. If there is additional stress in the home, find ways to give the child "fun" time.

Dealing with Death/Loss

Like adults, children need to grieve.

Like adults, children deal with their grief in different ways.

This could be grief due to the loss of a friend moving away, the loss of a parent during separation, the loss of their spot on a team, or the death of a pet or a person.

One may cry a lot, one child may talk a lot about their feelings or the loss, one child may withdraw.

Do not dismiss or minimize the grief. Normalize the grieving process. Validate the feelings of sadness, anger, confusion and loss. If it is important to your child, it needs to be important to you. Be comfortable with their grief. Support your child emotionally and let them know that the pain they feel will lessen over time. They will get through this. Teach them how they can get through the emotional pain; talking about their feelings, crying to let the pain out, and self-soothing such as pampering self and allowing self to experience joy and fun during the grieving process without guilt.

Loss of a Pet

If possible, do not let the death of a pet be a surprise. If the pet is old or ill, you need to prepare the child. Be honest and speak in age-appropriate terms.

Be honest with your child in a gentle way. If you need to euthanize your pet, explain it to the child. Allow them to say goodbye. It may or may not be appropriate for the child to be present while the pet is being euthanized. The child needs to be old enough and mature enough to make this choice, to fully understand what is happening, to be able to be calm and deal with their emotions so they can comfort the animal.

Do not tell your child the pet ran away when it died. They may remain hopeful and watch for the pet to return. Eventually they will discover the truth and find out you lied. This will break their trust in you. By telling them a lie, you are depriving them of their right to grieve.

Grieving a pet prepares your child to be able to grieve human deaths.

Share your happy memories of the pet. Talk about the pet. Find a child's book about the loss of a pet. Read it together for the first few days, and then if the child asks for it. The book provides your child with the opportunity to talk about the pet and their feelings.

Do not get a new pet until the child has processed feelings about the loss. Do not surprise your child with a new pet. Make the decision as a family when everyone is emotionally ready.

Dealing with the Death of a Friend or Family Member

The loss of a friend, aunt or uncle or grandparent can be very significant for your child, even if the person is seen infrequently.

It is good for your child to see that you are sad, to cry and express your feeling of loss. It is important to show that you are sad and grieving, but you will be okay.

Your child will watch you deal with the loss, and will likely model your grieving process. It is important for your child to understand that death is part of life. It is important to grieve and live at the same time.

Dealing with the Loss of a Sibling or Parent

It is very important to ensure the child's physical and emotional needs are met after the loss of a sibling or parent.

If you as the parent are deeply grieving, it is important to arrange for trusted people to meet the needs of your child, if you temporarily are not able.

Counselling may also be a healthy avenue of support for your grieving child.

It is very important that the remaining child does not feel that they are not as important or special as the child or parent that died.

Validating And Building Self-Esteem

Respect Your Child's Individuality

Your child is an individual; separate from you with different interests, skills and preferences.

Trying to make your child into a clone of yourself, or wanting your child to achieve what you wanted to achieve can make your child feel inadequate.

Encourage your child to pursue their own interests and goals.

Value your child for who they are and they will blossom.

Try Not to Expect Too Much or Too Little

Do not have unrealistic expectations of what your child can achieve. Parental expectations that are too high can make a child feel they are disappointing their parent, and that they do not measure up.

Do not expect too little of a child, especially a child with challenges, as that can lead to underperformance and self-esteem issues.

Be realistic. Provide encouragement and support without pressure. Provide some opportunities that ensure success and some that provide manageable challenge.

Do not limit your children. Do not squash their dreams. Give them encouragement and confidence that they can strive for and achieve whatever goals they work towards.

Spend One on One Time with Each Child

It is natural to feel that you have more in common with one child, and end up spending more time doing that activity together. It is important to find a way to bond with all your children to make them feel equally special. Not doing this could result in self-esteem issues – not feeling valued by the parent, not feeling good enough or enough.

Some children demand more attention due to their personality or special needs. Be sure to give special attention to the other children as well. Even if they seem fine with less attention, you need to ensure you are meeting their needs and they feel equally important or the lack of attention may manifest into issues later on.

Listen to Your Children

Try to understand what they feel and what they need. This allows your children to feel emotionally safe with you. This allows your children to be able to be open and honest with you without fear of judgement.

Don't assume you know what they are feeling or thinking. You may be surprised to find out how far off your assumption is from what they are really feeling or thinking.

Talk with Your Children in a Non-judgemental Way

If you are open and help guide your children to understand their thoughts and action, they will be more likely to talk to you, or come to you when in a difficult situation.

If you come across as judgemental or ridicule them, they will shut down.

If you are concerned about your children's behaviour or mental health, then seek help. Speak with your family doctor or obtain counselling for you and/or your children. This will help to support your children and help them to learn to work through problems, which will enhance their sense of self-esteem.

Understand that Each Child May Need a Different Approach Due to Their Different Personalities

You will notice your children have very different personalities, even as babies.

Each child may react differently to certain parenting styles.

For example, one child may do what is asked right away. Another child may ask many questions and have to understand why they need to do something.

One child may need only to be asked once, whereas the other child may need to be presented with several options and clear reasons why each would be beneficial.

One child may feel comfortable with well defined rules and limits. Another child may need more freedom and options.

The independent thinker may respond more to options and explanations.

It is important not to judge and label the children such as the "easy or good child", or the "challenging or difficult child".

The qualities in your child can end up being positive or negative, depending on how they are managed.

The "easy or good child" may excel in school and be praised by teachers, but may get taken advantage of by fellow students or become a follower due to people pleasing behaviours.

The independent thinker, sometimes called the "challenging or difficult child", may end up being an entrepreneur who developed a new ground breaking invention due to their inquisitiveness.

However, if that child was labelled a "difficult or a problem child", then the qualities may end up manifesting as negative aspects. Don't let that happen.

Value the unique personalities of each of your children.

Treat Your Child with Respect

This is how a child learns that they are worthy of respect.

This is how a child learns self-respect.

Respect includes how you use your words, facial expressions, and body language. Respect includes how you listen to what someone says instead of dismissing or talking over them. This includes using all above in a respectful manner with your child. You can still be a strong parent, setting and enforcing the rules and consequences, in a firm, kind and respectful manner.

A parent may have been taught that one needs to yell or be aggressive to get a child to listen. However, it is the consistency of rules and enforcement of appropriate consequences that gets the child to listen and understand that the parent means what they say.

Speak to Your Child Only in a Way That You Would Want Someone to Speak to You.

This includes your tone of voice, your words and your body language.

There are ways to be firm without being rude, disrespectful, demeaning or shaming.

There is no place for calling your children names or swearing at them.

Putting them down or shaming them **does not** teach them to be strong. It teaches them to feel that something is wrong with them.

This creates a pattern where they could end up in relationships where they are not treated well, as they become used to being put down and not feeling worthy.

Give Your Child the Gift of Self-Esteem

If by words and actions you show that your child is important and special to you, your child will feel that way inside. This is how self-esteem and self-worth is developed.

Telling your children, they are not good enough does not make them stronger, it makes them feel inadequate.

Make your child feel special by the words you say, how you treat them and how you make time for them.

Spend Quality Time Together.

Being with your children shows that you value them.

Show them that you enjoy spending time with them.

This is how they learn they are valuable and worthy of love.

Give Your Child the Gift of Self Confidence

Show confidence in your child's abilities and decisions.

This is how your child learns to be confident in their abilities and decisions.

Be an advocate for your child and teach them how to advocate for themselves in situations and relationships.

Advocate for resources and special services if your child has special needs. Reinforce extra help is positive as it helps build skill mastery which builds self confidence.

Set the example.
Be What You Ask
Your Kids to Be

Children Do What You Do, Not What You Tell Them To Do

If you want your child to be confident... be confident.

Remember they model your behaviour.

If you want your child to be positive...be positive.

If you want your child to be responsible...be responsible.

Your Values Will Likely Become Your Children's Values

Think carefully about your values and your actions and how these will impact your child's life.

Pay attention to your words and behaviours, as these will be repeated by your child.

How you treat others and yourself is how your child will treat others and themselves.

Model Happiness and Positivity

Laugh and have fun with your child. This teaches the child how to have fun and to enjoy life.

Develop a positive attitude. See the positive instead of the negative side of things. Approach situations with a positive outlook. It is a choice.

One is guaranteed to feel better inside if they choose positive words and a positive attitude, regardless of external situations.

Your child will model this positivity and happiness.

Respect Yourself

Children model your words and actions. If you minimize yourself, engage in negative self talk, or allow others to treat you disrespectfully, then your children eventually will mimic your behaviour.

Your children may start engaging in negative self talk, minimizing themselves or allowing others to treat them disrespectfully. Or it may have the opposite effect with your children starting to treat you or others disrespectfully.

Do and say what you want your children to do and say.

Be Honest

Children can usually sense or will find out when you are lying. This causes a lack of trust.

Be truthful, but give information in a way that allows your child to feel safe and protected, and can be understood at that age.

Be mindful that young children do not have the ability to screen what is and what is not appropriate to share with others. If you want something kept private, do not discuss it in front of them.

Be Reliable

Children need to know you will be there to have a sense of security. Be consistent in what you say or do to make your child's environment and routine safe and predictable.

Do What You Say

Children need to be able to count on you to feel safe. Children need to know their parents will do what they say, and will be there when they say. This provides a sense of security for the child.

Be the Parent (Do Not Discuss Adult Material with Your Children or Make Them Look after You)

Children are not emotionally equipped to deal with adult matters.

Children are not to be used as your emotional support or as your counsellor, even if they are teenagers and seem mature.

Children are not there to look after you emotionally. It is the other way around.

If your child is put in the role of emotional caregiver of you the parent, the child's feelings and needs will become secondary. The child will learn their feelings and needs are not as important as others. The child will likely choose relationships where they sacrifice their needs for the other person. This could lead to emotionally, physically, sexually or financially abusive relationships.

If you find yourself using emotional manipulation to get your child to spend time with you or look after you, then you need to stop and seek counselling.

If you need to speak to someone about your feelings, financial issues or relationship problems, then speak with a friend, an adult family member or a counsellor.

Do not speak with your child, your pre-teen or your teenager about your adult problems. They are not emotionally equipped to deal with adult problems, nor is it their role or responsibility.

You are there to look after your child. Your child is not there to look after you.

Love Your Child

Their ability to love themselves comes from your ability to make them feel loved.

Say I Love You

Say the actual words I love you. Children need to hear they are loved.

Show I Love You

Showing love includes the way you look at your child with love and appreciation. Showing love is saying loving, not hurtful things to your children. Showing love is being reliable and trustworthy. Showing love is meeting the child's basic physical needs and then also meeting your child's emotional needs.

Showing love includes giving affection – hugs and comfort.

Joint Parenting

How Do I Parent with My Partner?

The most important factor in joint parenting is to be on the same page. Both partners need to give the same message to the child. The partners need to support each other and make parenting decisions together.

If one parent says one thing and the other parent says something else, this creates confusion for the child. The child can also learn to manipulate their parents and play one off the other. This ends up negatively affecting the parents' relationship and actually negatively affects the child.

Part of the development of a child's self-esteem is having respect for the parents. If the child is able to manipulate the parents, the child will lose respect for the parents. Over time, if the disrespect and lack of parenting continues, it is likely the child will then stop respecting other adults (teachers, authority such as police and bosses). The child will then likely have difficulty learning how to work through frustration and be accountable for their behaviour. It is possible the child will start using substances such as drugs or alcohol as they have not learned there are consequences for their behaviour, or to accept responsibility for their behaviours and may develop impulse control issues. The eventual end result will be the child having a lack of respect for the self and a feeling of being lost and unfocused in life.

Be mindful of treatment of gender roles in parenting. For example, if a father puts the mother down and says things like "you're worthless, you can't do anything right", then the children may see the role of the female as reduced and lose respect for the mother and possibly females in general. The female child may grow up feeling useless and pick males that treat her badly. The male child may also grow up seeing the female as useless which will translate into his views of women and how he treats his partners.

If the mother says to the father you can't do anything right, now I have to do it over, the children may have a reduced opinion of the male.

It is important to be mindful of this also in same sex marriages. The way one partner treats the other will manifest in the child's treatment of self and others.

What if We are Separated or Divorced?

This is when parenting can become even more challenging. Separation often occurs when there are issues in a relationship. Separating the relationship issues from parenting can be very challenging; especially when one partner has been left, cheated on, or has been emotionally or physically abused.

It is important for the child to have a relationship and spend time with both parents – as long as there is not abuse involved. For healthy development a child needs to see their male and female role models in a positive light.

Adult issues such as child support payments, infidelity, and any relationship issues should **not** be discussed with your child. The adult topics need to be addressed by the adults.

The children are **not** to be used as pawns in an adult relationship. If adults are using the child to vent about the shortcomings of the other parent, or are withholding time with a parent due to anger over their failed relationship, this will only serve to hurt and emotionally scar the child.

Deal with your own anger, hurt and disappointment by attending counselling, not by involving a child. Seek professional support to best be able to deal with difficult situations for the sake of yourself and your child.

If you are dealing with a controlling, manipulative partner your resources will be counselling, knowing and utilizing your legal rights and contacting your local Children's Aid Society if emotional, sexual or physical abuse is involved.

It is important to consider that these types of claims are very serious. Making unfounded claims based on anger or fears about custody arrangements is not acceptable and is harmful to your children.

If your partner was emotionally abusive or controlling, then individual or group therapy may be required for you to develop coping strategies about how to deal with this ex partner for the benefit of the children. For example, counselling can help you look at family patterns that set you up to enter into an emotionally abusive relationship, and what patterns and relationship skills can be changed to effectively deal with/stop the manipulation and control. Counselling and day treatment programs will help you to develop the skills and coping mechanisms to deal with the situation.

If you and your ex partner are involved in a custody battle, it is important to remember the well-being of your child is the most important thing – not your anger or pain towards your ex. Do not use your child as a tool to manipulate or hurt your ex. This ends up hurting your child and eventually your relationship with your child.

Introducing a New Person Into My Child's Life

When you become involved with a new person, get to know who the person really is before introducing them into your child's life. If the person is trustworthy, then gradually introduce them into your child's life. You want to ensure the new partner is going to be around for the long-term to avoid any more hurt for your child.

Ensure your new partner has a similar approach to parenting and similar values, or your family will encounter many conflicts. Prior to moving in with a new partner discuss household rules and how they will be reinforced.

Remember to have one on one time with your children. They need this time to talk to you, to be with you and feel they are still important to you. Remember it will take time for your children to feel comfortable with a new person in your life. It is normal for your child to feel some level of concern or resentment that the new person is trying to replace mom or dad. Reassure your child the new partner is not replacing the parent. Listen to your children's concerns and validate, not dismiss them. Let them talk through their worries. Reassure them that you understand their feelings, you still love them and will keep them safe. If you continue to listen to a child and they feel safe to talk to you, they will be able to tell you if a new partner is doing something that is not healthy. Hear and address warning signals that your child is telling you. Your job is to keep your child safe, not to make sure you keep your relationship if there is something unhealthy going on.

Try to minimize any life changes with a new partner; for example, moving out of area away from your child's school, friends and extended family. If there are life changes as a result of your selected relationship, it is your role to ensure your child is emotionally validated and supported through the change.

What to Do If My Child is Sexually Abused?

Most importantly, support your child and reinforce that it was not their fault and keep your child safe.

It is common that people, regardless of age, who have been sexually abused carry a sense of shame or guilt. It is extremely important that the child understand that they are not in any way at all to blame.

It is important to ensure that the child is kept safe and away from the abuser, even if it is a family member. Wanting to attend family gatherings is not a valid excuse for failing to keep your child safe and away from the abuser. It is important to hold the abuser accountable for the abuse. If the abuser is in your home then the abuser needs to leave. If that is not possible then you and the child need to leave. Your child must not be made to leave alone. They need to know the abuse is not their fault. Sending them away makes them feel as if they did something wrong. The Children's Aid Society/police need to be informed to help ensure the child is protected and validated.

Ensure your child receives counselling from an agency that specializes in child counselling. Counselling for the parent is also recommended for support in dealing appropriately with the situation.

If a parent was in a situation where as a child they were sexually abused and their families denied or minimized the abuse, or did not protect the child, then the parent is less likely to be able to protect their own child from an abuser; even the same abuser. The parent will have been taught to minimize or avoid dealing with the abuse and may sweep it under the carpet as they have been taught. Again, this is when counselling for the parent will be necessary to avoid repeating the same unhealthy pattern.

In most places there is a duty to report abuse of a child. If you do not protect your child, an agency with that mandate may be called in to ensure your child is protected. If you continue not to protect your child, then legally your child can be removed from your home and your custody.

Parenting Summary

Imagine holding a baby in your arms. The job of the parent is to do everything for the baby; the basics - feed, change diapers, bathe, provide love and keep the child safe from harm.

As the baby transitions into a toddler the job of the parent is to continue to provide the basics and to allow the child to explore the environment while keeping the child safe. This allows the development of skills. For example, the child crawls on the floor and the parent prevents the child from sticking anything into an electrical socket.

As the toddler transitions into a child, the job of the parent is to continue to allow the child to explore the environment and to learn new skills – balance, coordination, decision making, learning right from wrong, that there are consequences for actions, etc.

This continues as the child transitions to pre-teen and teenage years, although it becomes more challenging. It becomes a delicate balance between keeping your child safe and allowing the freedom to learn and practice skills – learning how to develop healthy relationships, how to learn to stick to a task and complete it, how to develop a sense of pride and achievement, and how to separate self identity from others, etc.

As the teenager transitions into a young adult the role of the parent is to be available to provide advice and guidance. If everything is done for the teenager/young adult, this takes away the opportunity for learning and skill development and skill refinement which results in a sense of mastery and self confidence.

The role of the parent is to provide the child with the skills necessary to become a self-sufficient adult who is able to manage their own life and engage in healthy, loving relationships.

The role of the parent is to be a cheerleader; to encourage, support and provide confidence.

This is done with statements such as "you can do it, I am here to support you, it's okay if it is not perfect as you are just learning, I know you can do anything you set your mind to, I will be here to help you figure it out, it's okay that you are frustrated – I'll show you how to work through your frustration".

The role of the parent is to be a protector.

Protection comes in the role of supervision to ensure personal safety from accidents and physical, sexual and emotional harm from others.

The role of the parent is to be a role model.

Model the words and actions, including body language and facial expressions, that you want to see from your child.

The role of the parent is to be a guide and a teacher.

Guidance through life in terms of values and morals, teaching how to learn, how to manage emotions and conflict, how to problem solve and how to develop healthy relationship skills and select healthy friends and partners.

What to Do

Be honest, trustworthy, dependable.

Be consistent and fair when setting and reinforcing rules and guidelines with consequences.

Show your child they are important and loveable by spending time with them, telling them and showing them that they are important and loved.

Model words and behaviours you want from your child. Be accountable and hold your child accountable.

Be available as a cheerleader, a guide and a mentor.

Use humour and try to make things fun.

Be present, reliable and loving.

Say positive things to your child. Say positive things about your child.

Model Positivity. Adopt and teach a positive outlook.

Be a healthy role model.

Get counselling when needed.

Be the parent. Teach and demonstrate how to attend to emotions and problem-solve through any situation with calmness and respect.

What Not to Do

Do not swear at your child.

Do not yell at your child in rage.

Do not hit your child.

Do not say bad things about your child in front of your child or others.

Do not tell a child they do not measure up, or can't do anything right.

Do not tell your child they are a loser, or no good.

Do not put your child down for not doing something right, instead of showing them how to do it right.

Do not look at your child in ways that are dismissive or demeaning.

Do not put the other parent down in front of the child.

Do not talk about adult matters around your child.

Do not use your child as your counsellor.

Do not ignore your child.

Do not allow your child to be harmed emotionally, physically or sexually by you or anyone else.

Conclusion

This has been an introduction to the some of the basic rules of parenting. This book is meant to provide a basic framework and set you on a path.

This book is intended to give you a quick, visual overview that you can pull out and skim over quickly anytime. When you feel stressed with your child, or at your limit, just take a few deep breaths and pull out this book. It will set you back on track.

If your child is having new or ongoing problems seek help. You can obtain counselling to help you determine options and skills for dealing with situations. Obtain counselling for your child. There is no shame in seeking help. Professionals are there for a reason. They are trained to provide support and therapeutic intervention.

For more details such as information on age-appropriate limits and consequences that can be used, please continue your parenting journey by reading more parenting books.

Take time to enjoy the experience. Remember no one is perfect. When we admit our mistakes and correct them, we are teaching our child how to do the same. We can accept that we don't have to be perfect. We are perfectly imperfect. We can be comfortable and proud of our individuality. Then our child learns to feel the same.

Just keep following the Parenting Basics and breath!

And remember to take time to be fully present with your children and enjoy the experience because in no time they are all grown up.

Enjoy Your Parenting Journey!

Addendum

Please note that the material presented here is not new. It will be found in any parenting book. The purpose is to present the basic principles that work, in a very simple way that is easy to understand and apply.

Thank you to my sister Suzanne for her invaluable feedback.

Thank you to my mom and dad for their love and support.

Thank you to my stepmother for taking such good care of me when my condo exploded.

Thank you to my friend Cheryl for her guidance and leading me to new experiences, to Anita for her friendship, to Ilse for always lending a helping hand, and to all my beloved extended family and friends.

Printed in the United States
by Baker & Taylor Publisher Services